SYMBOLS OF AMERICA

THE UNITED STATES FLAG

KIM THOMPSON

NorwoodHouse Press

Cataloging-in-Publication Data

Names: Thompson, Kim.
Title: The United States flag / Kim Thompson.
Description: Buffalo, NY : Norwood House Press, 2026. | Series: Symbols of America | Includes glossary and index.
Identifiers: ISBN 9781978575820 (pbk.) | ISBN 9781978575837 (library bound) | ISBN 9781978575844 (ebook)
Subjects: LCSH: Flags--United States--Juvenile literature.
Classification: LCC CR113.T466 2026 | DDC 929.9'20973--dc23

Published in 2026 by
Norwood House Press
2544 Clinton Street
Buffalo, NY 14224

Designer: Rhea Magaro

Photo credits: Cover, p. 1 Collins Unlimited/Shutterstock.com; p. 3 Katarzyna Hurova/Shutterstock.com; p. 4 Azlan Stock/Shutterstock.com; p. 5 MargJohnsonVA/Shutterstock.com; pp. 6, 7, 11, 12 Library of Congress; p. 8 Everett Collection/Shutterstock.com; p. 9 S. Vincent/Shutterstock.com; pp. 10, 14, 17 Dennis MacDonald/Shutterstock.com; p. 13 Andrey_Popov/Shutterstock.com; p. 15 Adam Parent/Shutterstock.com; p. 16 sirtravelalot/Shutterstock.com; p. 18 Bill Perry/Shutterstock.com; p. 19 Prostock-studio/Shutterstock.com; p. 20 mr_tigga/Shutterstock.com;

Printed in the United States of America

CPSIA compliance information: Batch #CSNHP26: For further information contact Norwood House Press at 1-800-237-9932.

TABLE OF CONTENTS

THE UNITED STATES FLAG

It waves over schools and government buildings. It flies on Flag Day and other holidays. It marks voting places on Election Day. It is the American flag.

The flag has many nicknames. It is called Old Glory, the Stars and Stripes, and the Star-Spangled Banner.

HOW IT BEGAN

No one knows for sure how the first American flag was created. A legend says it was sewn by a woman named Betsy Ross around 1776.

In 1777, the U.S. was a new country. Leaders approved a flag design. It had 13 red and white stripes. It had 13 white stars on a blue field to represent a new **constellation**.

In 1814, a huge flag survived an epic battle. British troops attacked Fort McHenry for over 24 hours. But the flag still waved.

Seeing that flag led Francis Scott Key to write "The Star-Spangled Banner." The flag is on display at the National Museum of American History in Washington, D.C.

As America changed, the flag did too. The last time the flag changed was 1960. A 50th star was added when Hawaii became a state.

Explorers have carried the flag to new places. It was planted at the North Pole in 1909. In 1963, it flew at the top of Mount Everest. In 1969, it was raised on the moon.

A SYMBOL OF AMERICA

The flag's 13 stripes represent the 13 **colonies** that declared **independence** from Great Britain. The stars represent the 50 states.

The color red stands for **valor** and bravery.
White stands for **purity** and innocence.
Blue stands for **vigilance** and justice.

The flag must be handled with respect. It should fly higher than other flags around it. A ceremony may be held when the flag is raised at sunrise and lowered at sunset.

The flag should never be displayed upside down. It should never touch the ground. The flag is flown at half-staff in times of national tragedy and **mourning**.

When the flag passes by in a parade, Americans stand. They remove hats. They place their right hands over their hearts.

Americans say “The **Pledge** of Allegiance” to show respect for the flag and **loyalty** to their country.

The U.S. flag is a **symbol** of America. Both things have survived wars and other challenges. Both have changed over time. Both stand for freedom.

Can you think of other ways that the American flag is like the United States?

SPOT THE SYMBOL

If you look closely, you will see stars and stripes on many things related to America. They are on the Great Seal of the U.S. They are on the 50 dollar bill. Many stamps show American flags.

GLOSSARY

colonies (KAH-luh-neez): territories that have been settled by people from another country and that are also controlled by that country

constellation (kahn-stuh-LAY-shuhn): a group of stars in the night sky

independence (in-di-PEN-duhns): freedom; self-rule

loyalty (LOI-uhl-tee): faithfulness, devotion, and friendship

mourning (MOR-ning): sadness because someone has died

pledge (plej): a serious promise

purity (PYOOR-uh-tee): not dirty, polluted, or guilty of wrongdoing

symbol (SIM-buhl): an object or design that stands for, suggests, or represents something else

valor (VAL-ur): great courage, especially in battle

vigilance (VIJ-uh-luhnts): care and watchfulness; always guarding and protecting

THINKING QUESTIONS

1. What are some nicknames for the American flag?
2. What do the stars and stripes represent?
3. What do the colors of the flag represent?
4. What inspired the song "The Star-Spangled Banner"?
5. How can people show respect for the flag?

INDEX

ABOUT THE AUTHOR

Kim Thompson is a teacher and writer from Columbus, Ohio. She is an American history buff. She loves to travel to look at statues, monuments, and museums. She thinks it would be fun to do a scavenger hunt to search for symbols of the United States.